DISCOVERING AFRICA

WEST

AFRICA

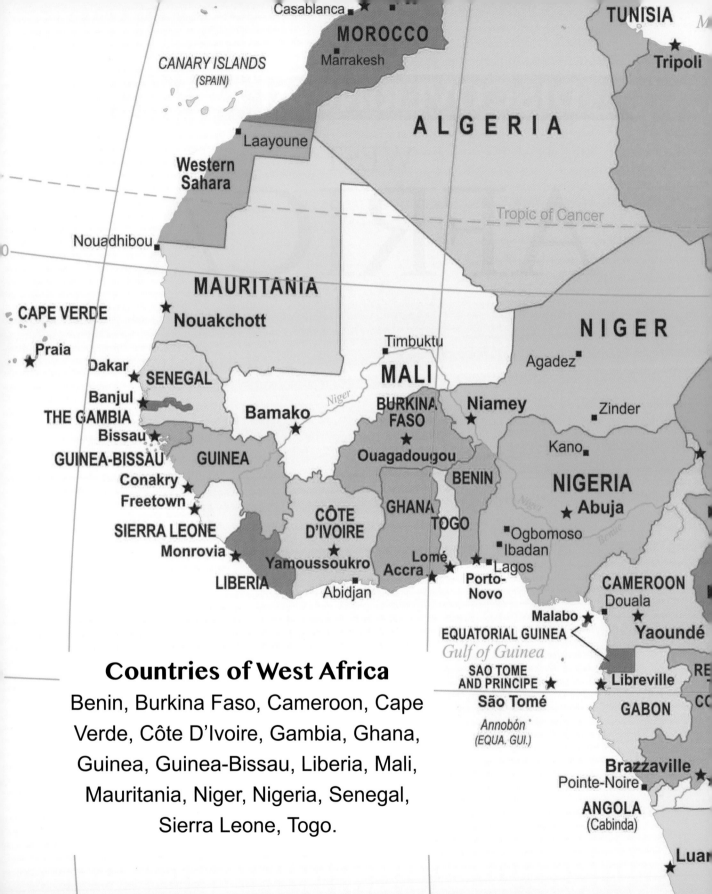

Countries of West Africa

Benin, Burkina Faso, Cameroon, Cape Verde, Côte D'Ivoire, Gambia, Ghana, Guinea, Guinea-Bissau, Liberia, Mali, Mauritania, Niger, Nigeria, Senegal, Sierra Leone, Togo.

DISCOVERING AFRICA

WEST
AFRICA

Annelise Hobbs

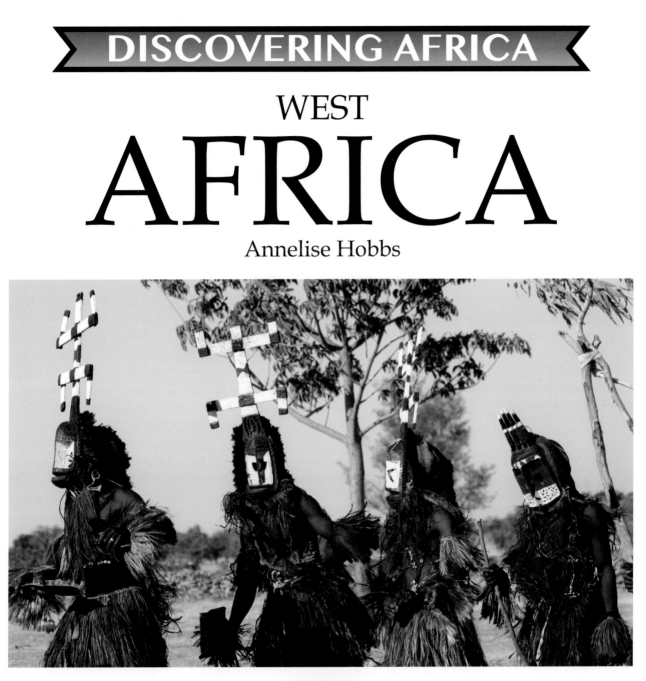

MASON CREST

Mason Crest
450 Parkway Drive, Suite D
Broomall, PA 19008
www.masoncrest.com

Cataloging-in-Publication Data on file with the Library of
Congress.

Printed and bound in the United States of America.

First printing
9 8 7 6 5 4 3 2 1

ISBN: 978-1-4222-3720-5
Series ISBN: 978-1-4222-3715-1
ebook ISBN: 978-1-4222-8071-3
ebook series ISBN: 978-1-4222-8066-9

Produced by Regency House Publishing Limited
The Manor House
High Street
Buntingford
Hertfordshire
SG9 9AB
United Kingdom

www.regencyhousepublishing.com

Text copyright © 2017 Regency House Publishing
Limited/Annelise Hobbs

CONTENTS

KEY ICONS TO LOOK FOR:

Words to Understand: These words with their easy-to-understand definitions will increase the reader's understanding of the text, while building vocabulary skills.

Sidebars: This boxed material within the main text allows readers to build knowledge, gain insights, explore possibilities, and broaden their perspectives by weaving together additional information to provide realistic and holistic perspectives.

Text-Dependent Questions: These questions send the reader back to the text for more careful attention to the evidence presented there.

BENIN

Benin is located between Nigeria and Togo, and has a short coastline on the Bight of Benin.

Known as Dahomey until 1975, it was once one of Africa's most powerful kingdoms, larger than at present and the traditional birthplace of **voodoo**. In fact, many such tribal kingdoms existed in Africa until the mid 19th century, when France assumed control. It was captured by the Portuguese in the 16th century, who were expelled by the Dutch in 1642 when it developed a flourishing slave trade, mainly with Brazil. France signed a treaty in 1851, making Dahomey a protectorate in

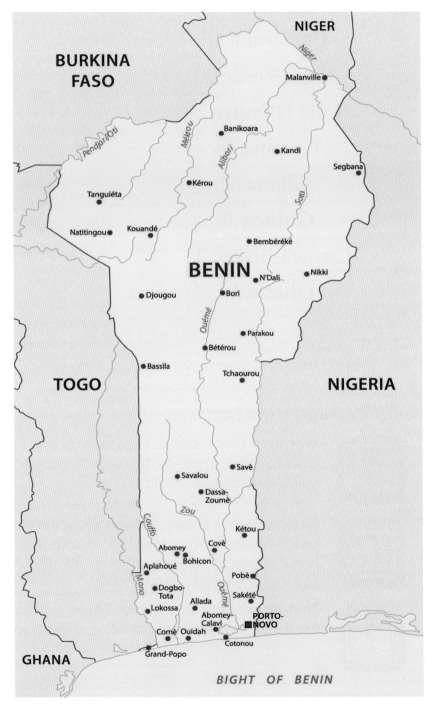

OPPOSITE LEFT: Gezo was a king of the Kingdom of Dahomey, in present-day Benin, from 1818 until 1858.

OPPOSITE RIGHT: A map of Benin.

BELOW: An engraving depicting armed Dahomey women, accompanied by the king, at war in 1793.

Words to Understand

Corruption: Dishonest or illegal behavior especially by people in power such as government officials or police officers.

Coup: The sudden overthrow of a government by a usually small group of persons, in or previously in positions of authority, usually the military.

Voodoo: Originating in Africa, a type of religion involving magic and the worship of spirits.

1863. It became a colony in 1872, becoming part of French West Africa in 1904. In 1960 it became an independent republic outside the French community. A number of military **coups** followed, and the country eventually adopted Marxist-Leninism in 1974, after which it became Benin, though it should not be confused with the former African kingdom of that name.

A multi-party democracy was established in 1991. President Mathieu Kerekou, the head of state since 1996, stepped down at the end of his second term in 2006, and was

Béhanzin

Béhanzin (1844–1906) was King of Dahomey, modern-day Benin. Upon taking the throne, he changed his name from Kondo, the shark. He succeeded his father, Glélé, and ruled from 1889–1894. Béhanzin was Abomey's last independent ruler established through traditional power structures. He led the national resistance during the Dahomey War in which French were eventually victorious, and in 1894, Béhanzin surrendered himself to French General Alfred Dodds, without signing any formal surrender or treaty. He lived out the remainder of his life in exile in Martinique and Algeria. After his death, his remains were returned to Abomey.

succeeded by Thomas Yayi Boni, a political outsider and independent. Yayi began a high-profile fight against corruption and strongly promoted Benin's economic growth. He was re-elected in 2011 for a second term. The current president, Patrice Talon was elected in March 2016. Known as the "King of Cotton" for his involvement in the cotton industry, he ran as an independent candidate.

Nowadays, there is little industry in Benin, but it is hoped that the architectural remnants of its glorious past as the Kingdom of Dahomey, as well as its wildlife parks, will continue to attract visitors to its shores.

OPPOSITE ABOVE: Congress Palace, Cotonou.

OPPOSITE BELOW: Statue of King Béhanzin in Abomey.

ABOVE: Men dressed for the ceremonial mask dance (*Egungun*), a traditional voodoo dance performed by the Yorbuba people of Benin and Nigeria.

Text-Dependent Questions

1. Who was the last king of Dahomey?

2. What year did Dahomey become part of French West Africa?

3. Who became president of Benin in 2016?

BURKINA FASO

Known as Upper Volta until 1984, Burkina Faso is an inland state of West Africa, situated north of Ghana. The terrain is mostly flat with undulating plains; hills lie in the west and south-east. There is recurrent drought.

The people belong either to the largest Voltaic group, or the Bobo. The former includes the Mossi, who

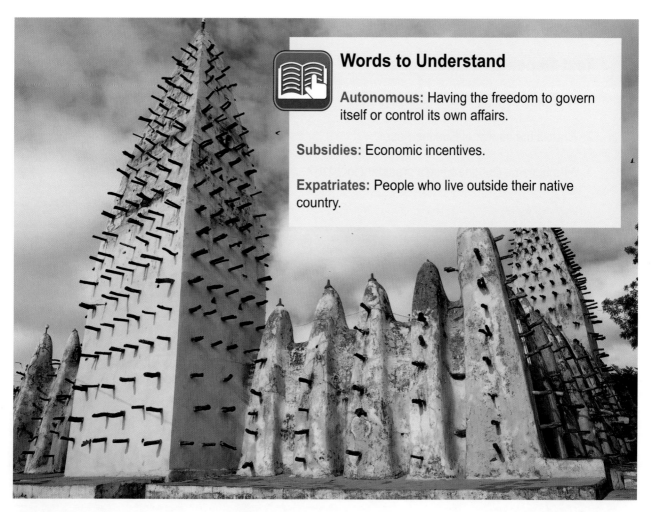

Words to Understand

Autonomous: Having the freedom to govern itself or control its own affairs.

Subsidies: Economic incentives.

Expatriates: People who live outside their native country.

OPPOSITE ABOVE: Resistance to the French invasion at Bobo-Dioulasso in 1892.

OPPOSITE: A map of Burkina Faso.

ABOVE: Grand Mosque of Bobo-Dioulasso.

originally established small kingdoms in the region in around 1100, including that of the capital Ouagadougou. Annexed by France in 1896 it became **autonomous** outside the French Community in 1960, following which there was a long period of military rule, interrupted in 1992 by the first multi-party ballots since 1978. President Blaise Compaoré won every election until 1987 when in 2014 he stepped aside following massive protests against plans to extend his rule. A transitional government took charge. In 2015, after a brief period of instabilty, former Prime Minister Roch Marc Christian Kaboré won the presidential election.

In 2016 Islamists attacked a hotel and cafe frequented by the French military and other **expatriates**, killing 29 people.

Text-Dependent Questions

1. What was Burkina Faso's original name?

2. What is the capital of Burkina Faso?

3. Who became Burkina Faso's president in 2015?

Burkina Faso is a poor country and most of its people scratch a living from the soil. Cotton is the main cash crop and the government has joined with three other cotton-producing countries in the region, Mali, Niger, and Chad, in persuading the World Trade Organization that fewer **subsidies** should be given to their competitors.

Despite hardship, Burkina Faso is a fascinating and colorful country and its people are cheerful if fatalistic.

LEFT: The strange and unique rock formations of the Domes de Fabedougou have been sculpted by erosion.

BELOW: Cascades de Karfiguéla near Banfora are a series of waterfalls appearing along a stretch of the Komoé River.

CAMEROON

Located between Equatorial Guinea and Nigeria, Cameroon has a coastline on the Bight of Biafra. The terrain is mixed, with a coastal plain, a **dissected** plateau in the center, mountains in the west, and plains in the north. Cameroon is one of the most culturally diverse nations in Africa. Bantu speakers predominate along the coast, as does the Islamic faith.

Words to Understand

Dissected: Separated by erosion into many closely spaced crevices or gorges on the surface of a plateau.

Mandate: A commission given to a nation to administer the government and affairs of a former territory or colony.

Protectorate: The relationship of a strong state or authority over a weaker state or territory that it protects and partly controls.

LEFT: Paul Biya is Cameroon's current President.

ABOVE: Traditional mud houses in the Mandara mountains. Volcanic in origin, they extend about 120 miles (193km) along the northern part of the border between Cameroon and Nigeria.

RIGHT: A map of Cameroon.

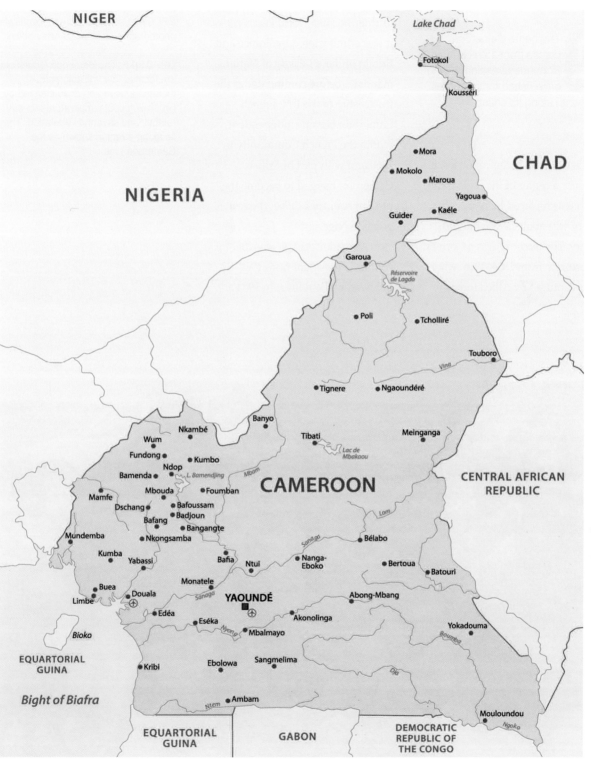

The name Cameroon comes from 15th century Portuguese explorers who once fished for camarões (prawns) along its coast.

Like other African countries, it was once a center of the slave trade, which was replaced by ivory when slavery was abolished in the 19th century. The territory was a German **protectorate** from 1884–1916, when it was captured by Allied forces during the First World War. Post-war it was administered by France and Britain under a League of Nations **mandate**, before coming under the trusteeship of the UN. French Cameroun became independent within the French Community in 1960 and with part of British Cameroon merged to become the present country in 1961, the rest going to Nigeria.

Ahmadou Ahidjo was the country's president from 1960–82, followed by Paul Biya. In 1984 a

BELOW: Cameroonian school children photographed with a US Army officer.

OPPOSITE: The Bamenda Grassfields are located in a volcanic and mountainous region characterized by high relief, cool temperatures, heavy rainfall, and savanna vegetation. They lie along a region known as the Cameroon Line.

failed coup led to many executions. Biya was re-elected in 1992 and has been president ever since.

Cameroon is one of tropical Africa's richer nations, though its wealth is unevenly distributed. The country is mostly agricultural, but it has ample oil reserves and other mineral resources, including gold and bauxite.

Text-Dependent Questions

1. What is the capital city of Cameroon?

2. Where did Cameroon get its name from?

3. What are the Bamenda Grassfields and what prominent geological feature can be found there?

CAPE VERDE

A republic consisting of an archipelago of 15 volcanic islands in the North Atlantic Ocean, Cape Verde is strategically placed on shipping routes 350 miles (565km) west of Cape Vert in Senegal, the most westerly point in Africa. It is divided into two groupings, the Leeward and the Windward Islands, and the terrain is steep and rugged.

Previously uninhabited, the islands were settled by the Portuguese in the 15th century as a base for the slave trade, and later as an important supply stop for transatlantic shipping. They became an overseas territory of Portugal in 1951 and independent in 1975.

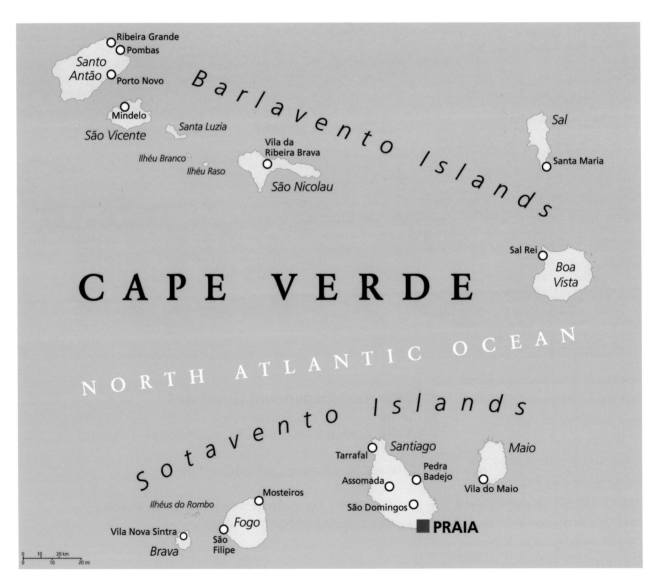

OPPOSITE: A map the the Cape Verde islands showing the Windward (Barlavento) Islands and the Windward (Sotavento) Islands.

BELOW: Praia is the capital of Cape Verde and is situalted on the island of Santiago.

Words to Understand

Democratic goverment: A system of government by the people, through elected representatives.

Strategically: Useful or important in achieving a plan or strategy.

Transatlantic: Concerning countries on both sides of the Atlantic Ocean.

Historically, the name "Cape Verde" has been used in English for the archipelago and, since independence in 1975, for the country. In 2013, the Cape Verdean government determined that the Portuguese term "Cabo Verde" would henceforth be used for official purposes, such as at the United Nations.

Text-Dependent Questions

1. How many Islands make up the archipelago of Cape Verde?

2. Who were the first to settle on Cape Verde?

3. Who is Cape Verde's president?

OPPOSITE ABOVE: Cape Verdean, former Prime Minister José Maria Neves meets with the US Secretary of Defense Chuck Hagel in 2013.

OPPOSITE BELOW: Tarrafal beach, Santiago island.

ABOVE: Santo Antão, the largest of the Barlavento islands is entirely made up of volcanic material.

Cape Verde has one of the most stable **democratic governments** in Africa. In 2011, in the most recent election, Jorge Carlos Fonseca was elected president to become the fourth president since Cape Verde's independence. The current prime minister is José Ulisses de Pina Correia e Silva.

Poor soil and lack of surface water limits agriculture, so that much of the food, apart from fish, must be imported. In an effort to take advantage of its proximity to cross-Atlantic sea and air lanes, the government has embarked on a major expansion of its port and airport capabilities. Cape Verde has significant co-operation with Portugal at every level of the economy, which has led it to link its currency first to the Portuguese escudo and, in 1999, to the euro.

CÔTE D'IVOIRE

A republic on the Gulf of Guinea, Côte d'Ivoire has borders with Liberia, Guinea, Mali, Burkina Faso, and Ghana. The heavily-forested coastal plain ascends steeply to a central plateau and mountains in the north-west, in an extension of the Guinea Highlands. The south-east coast is an area of enclosed lagoons, on one of which stands the former capital of Abidjan, which is also the chief port, while further along, rocky cliffs line the south-western coast.

Portuguese explorers visited the area in the late 15th century, but

various European traders, in search of slaves and ivory, wrangled over its possession. It became a French protectorate when France secured trading rights on the coast in 1842, then occupied the interior from 1882. It became part of French West Africa in 1904.

Ivory Coast gained full independence in 1960, though French is still the official language to this day. Its first president, Félix Houphoët-Boigny, was Africa's longest-serving leader, having held the post for 33 years until his death in 1993. He was succeeded by Henri Konan Bédié, who was deposed in a military coup led by General Robert Guei.

OPPOSITE ABOVE: Louis Gustave Binger of French West Africa in 1892, treaty signing with Famienkro leaders claiming Côte D'Ivoire for France.

OPPOSITE BELOW: The port town of Abidjan.

BELOW: A map of Côte D'Ivoire.

Words to Understand

Dispute: To argue about something.

Independence: The time when a country or region gains political freedom from outside control.

Predecessor: A person who had a job or position before someone else.

LEFT: A White House reception on May 22, 1962. Côte d'Ivoire President Félix Houphouët-Boigny, his wife Marie-Thérèse Houphouët-Boigny, US President John F. Kennedy and First Lady Jacqueline Kennedy.

BELOW: Catholic Basilica of Our Lady of Peace in the capital Yamoussoukro. Lebanese architect Pierre Fakhoury took inspiration from St. Peter's Basilica in the Vatican City, Rome.

Laurent Gbagbo became president in 2000, though the result of the election was **disputed** and civil unrest followed in its wake. In 2002, an armed rebellion split the nation in two. Since then, peace deals have alternated with renewed violence as the country has slowly edged its way towards a political resolution to the conflict. Alassane Ouattara has been in power since his **predecessor**, Laurent Gbagbo, was forcibly removed from office after refusing to accept Mr Ouattara's internationally recognized victory in the November 2010 election. In 2015, Mr Ouattara won a second five-year term.

Agriculture employs two-thirds of the population and accounts for 50 percent of the country's exports.

Bongo

The Bongo (*Tragelaphus eurycerus*) is a herbivorous, mostly nocturnal, forest ungulate. It is among the largest of the African forest antelope species and is native to Côte D'Ivoire.

Côte d'Ivoire is the world's largest exporter of cocoa beans and a large producer of coffee. Its offshore oil and gas production has resulted in substantial crude oil exports and provides sufficient natural gas to allow electricity exports to Ghana, Togo, Benin, Mali, and Burkina Faso.

Text-Dependent Questions

1. Name one of Côte d'Ivoire's main ports?

2. Who was Côte d'Ivoire's first president?

3. What year did Côte d'Ivoire become part of French West Africa?

GAMBIA

A country on the coast of West Africa, and the smallest in Africa, Gambia consists of a narrow strip of territory 20 miles (32km) wide and extending 200 miles (320km) inland on both sides of the River Gambia. Apart from its coastline, it is totally encompassed

by Senegal. The river has always attracted visitors to its magnificent estuary and **meandering** waterways, and it supports a rich variety of birds, fish, and mammals.

Portuguese ships visited Gambia in the 15th century, but British traders first came to the area nearly 100 years later, when a settlement was established. It was created a

Words to Understand

Commonwealth: A voluntary association of 53 independent and sovereign states.

Integration: Incorporation as equals into a society or an organization of individuals of different groups.

Meandering: A turn or winding of a waterway.

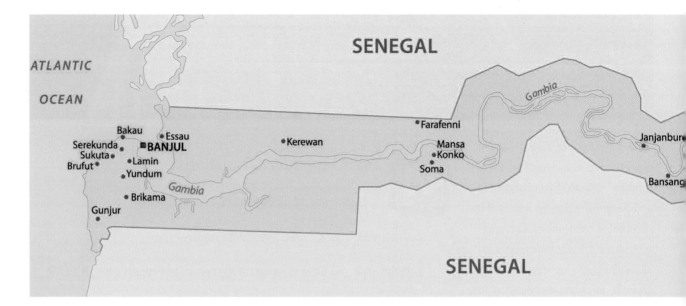

THE GAMBIA

Gambia
Allunhari
Gambissara
Basse
Santa Su
Sabi
Garowol

OPPOSITE ABOVE: Tropical forest along the Gambia river.

LEFT: A map of Gambia.

ABOVE: The Wassu stone circles are situated along the northern bank of the Gambia river. This sacred site has been declared by UNESCO as a World Heritage Site. These fascinating monuments are well-visited by students, geologists, historians, archaeologists, and tourists.

Stone Circles of Senegambia

The Senegambian stone circles are usually divided into four large sites: Sine Ngayene and Wanar in Senegal, and Wassu and Kerbatch in the central river region in Gambia. It is generally accepted that the monuments were built between the third century BC and the sixteenth century AD. Archaeologists have discovered human burials, pottery, and metals at the sites, as well as jewelry and spears. The construction of the stone monuments provide evidence that they were made by a well-organized and prosperous society, and that the stones were extracted from the ground using iron tools.

British colony in 1843, became an independent member of the **Commonwealth** in 1965, when Dawda Jawara became prime minister, and achieved full independence in 1970. From 1982, Gambia, with Senegal, formed the federation of Senegambia, which lasted only until 1989, when Gambia declined further **integration**. In 1992 Jawara was re-elected for a fifth term and in 1994 was overthrown in a military coup, led by Yahya Jammeh, chairman of the junta from 1994–96. Jammeh was elected president in 1996, but his regime was accused of political repression. However, there was a nominal return to civilian rule in 1997. In 2001, Jammeh lifted the ban on opposition parties and was subsequently re-elected. Jammeh was elected again in 2011 for a fourth term. On the morning of December 30, 2014, an attempt was made to oust President Jammeh in a coup which failed when palace guards fought back against their attackers.

Gambia has no significant mineral resources and has a limited agricultural base, most of the population relying on their own crops and livestock for subsistance. The processing of peanuts for export, fish, and hides is carried out in a limited way, but tourism is becoming increasingly important.

OPPOSITE ABOVE: A traditional stone building marked for the 2013 census in Banjul, the capital of Gambia.

OPPOSITE BELOW: The West African Crocodile (*Crocodylus suchus*) is native to Gambia.

ABOVE: The Western Red-billed Hornbill (*Tockus kempi*) is found in Senegal, Gambia, southern Mauritania, and western Mali.

Text-Dependent Questions

1. What industry is becoming important to Gambia's economy?

2. What country almost completely surrounds Gambia?

3. What is the name given to the stone circles found on the banks of the Gambia river?

GHANA

Ghana has land borders with Côte d'Ivoire in the west, Burkina Faso in the north, and Togo in the east, with a coastline bordering the Gulf of Guinea and the Atlantic Ocean. It is a mostly low-lying country, parts of which are irrigated to make them more productive, with a dissected forested plateau occupying the center and

Words to Understand

Dictatorial: Used to describe a person who tries to control other people in a forceful and unfair way.

Pan-African: A movement for the political union of all the African nations.

Subsistence: (Agricuture) A type of farming in which all the produce is consumed by the farmer and his family.

LEFT AND ABOVE: The Kwame Nkrumah Memorial Park in Accra is dedicated to Ghana's first president.

OPPOSITE: A map of Ghana.

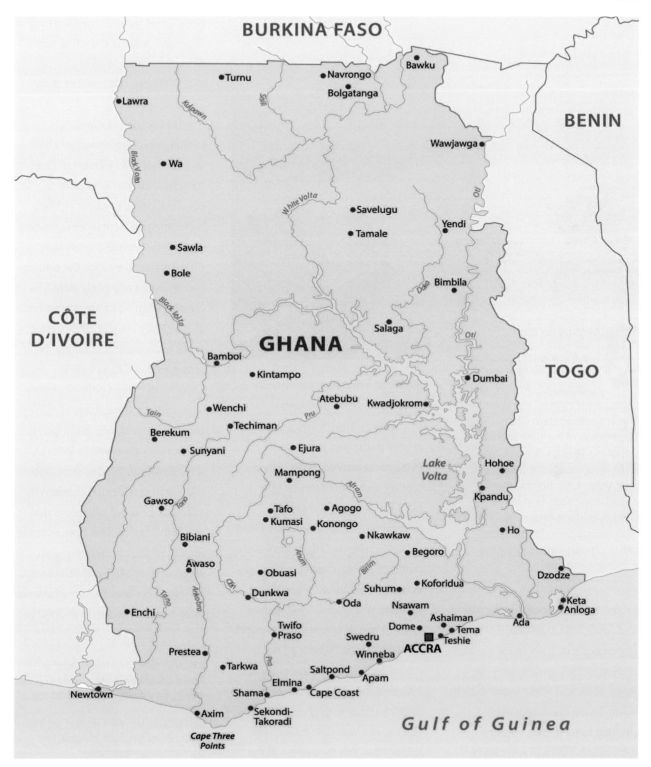

BURKINA FASO

BENIN

TOGO

CÔTE
D'IVOIRE

GHANA

Gulf of Guinea

Lawra

Turnu

Navrongo

Bawku

Bolgatanga

Wawjawga

Wa

Kulpawn

Sisili

Black Volta

White Volta

Oti

Savelugu

Tamale

Yendi

Sawla

Bole

Daka

Bimbila

Black Volta

Salaga

Oti

Bamboi

Kintampo

Atebubu

Kwadjokrom

Dumbai

Tain

Wenchi

Pru

Techiman

Lake
Volta

Hohoe

Berekum

Sunyani

Ejura

Mampong

Afram

Kpandu

Gawso

Tano

Tafo

Agogo

Kumasi

Konongo

Nkawkaw

Ho

Bibiani

Begoro

Dzodze

Awaso

Afram

Obuasi

Suhum

Koforidua

Keta
Anloga

Enchi

Tano

Ankobra

Ofin

Dunkwa

Oda

Birim

Nsawam

Ashaiman

Ada

Prestea

Twifo
Praso

Swedru

Dome

Tema

Teshie

ACCRA

Winneba

Tarkwa

Pra

Saltpond

Apam

Newtown

Shama

Elmina

Cape Coast

Axim

Sekondi-
Takoradi

*Cape Three
Points*

Akosombo Dam

The Akosombo Dam, also known as the Akosombo Hydroelectric Project, is a hydroelectric dam on the Volta river in south-eastern Ghana. The construction of the dam flooded part of the Volta river basin, and led to the subsequent creation of Lake Volta. Lake Volta is the largest man-made lake in the world by surface area. One important purpose for the dam was to provide electricity for the aluminium industry.

extending to the south. To the east and south lies Lake Volta, one of the largest artificial lakes in the world, created in 1965 by damming the River Volta, and which runs north to south. In the north, recurrent drought has a serious effect on agriculture, which in any case is mostly at a domestic **subsistence** level throughout the country.

Various African kingdoms existed in the area before the Portuguese arrived in the 15th century and named the area the Gold Coast, on account of its mineral wealth. It came under Dutch occupation in the 17th century and a center of the slave trade, which was eventually abolished when the Europeans retreated, leaving the Ashanti people to reclaim their land. The Gold Coast became a British colony in 1874, but it was not until 1901 that the war-like Ashanti lost their kingdom to the British. In 1957, Ghana, as it was now called, was formed through the merger of the Gold Coast with the trust territory of Togoland, making it the first sub-Saharan country to gain independence as a member of the Commonwealth.

Dr. Kwame Nkrumah, a prominent commentator on Third World affairs and pioneer of **Pan-African** socialism, first came to power as prime minister in 1952, becoming president in 1960. As time went on he became increasingly **dictatorial**, and by 1964 the country had become a one-party state. His colorful reign was brought to a end by a military coup in 1966. A long series of coups resulted in the suspension of Ghana's 1979 constitution, when political parties were banned, though a new constitution restoring multi-party politics was approved in 1992. Lt. Jerry Rawlings, head of state since 1981, won presidential elections in 1992 and 1996, but was prevented under the constitution from running for a third term in 2000. He was succeeded, in a free and fair election, by John Agyekum Kufuor who went on to win a second term in 2004. In

ABOVE: Akosombo Hydroelectric Power Station on the Volta river supplies energy for industry and domestic use.

OPPOSITE: Umbrella Rock in the Yilo Krobo District, outside of Accra, is a popular tourist destination.

2007 a new president, John Atta Mills was elected, but died in 2012. In the same year, John Mahama became interim head of state, but went on to an election victory.

Ghana is well-endowed with natural resources, that include gold, cocoa, and timber (the main sources of foreign exchange), silver, industrial diamonds, bauxite, manganese, fish, rubber, hydro-electricity, petroleum, salt, and limestone. Even so, it remains dependent on outside aid and technical assistance.

Text-Dependent Questions

1. What is the name of Ghana's largest man-made lake?

2. Who was Ghana's first prime minister and president?

3. How is electricity generated at the Akosombo Dam?

GUINEA

Its base bordering the Atlantic Ocean, the Republic of Guinea then curves to form land borders with Guinea-Bissau, Senegal, and Mali to the north and north-east, the Côte d'Ivoire to the south-east, Liberia to the south, and Sierra Leone to the west. There are mangrove swamps along part of the **alluvial** coastal plain, which

Words to Understand

Alluvial: Made up of or found in the materials that are left by the water of rivers, floods, etc.

Democratic: Based on a form of government in which the people choose leaders by voting.

Repressive: To control (someone or something) by force.

OPPOSITE: A map of Guinea.

ABOVE: The town of Mali or Maliville in the north of the country. Not to be confused with the country of Mali.

RIGHT: Ahmed Sékou Touré (1922–1984) was a Guinean political leader. He was elected as the first president of Guinea, serving from 1958 to his death in 1984. Touré was one of the primary Guinean nationalists involved in gaining independence from France. His regime was repressive, crushing all political opposition in his path.

includes the capital, Conakry. This rises to the dense forests of Fouta Djallon in the north-west. In the north-east is an area of tropical savanna, while to the south the Guinea highlands rise to a height of 5,748 feet (1752m) at Mount Nimba.

Guinea was the site of African empires that reached their zenith and then fell, such as those of Ghana, Sosso, and Mali. The Portuguese developed a trade in slaves centered on Guinea in the

16th century. Fulani Arabs established a Muslim state from 1735 until France gained control from 1849, following a series of wars, with the colony becoming French Guinea in 1890. Guinea gained independence from France in 1958, when it turned towards the Soviet Union.

The first president, Ahmed Sékou Touré, headed a **repressive** regime, crushing all political opposition in his path. As a result, thousands were tortured, killed, or disappeared. A military coup followed Touré's death in 1984, when power was seized by Lansana Conté, who abandoned socialism, released political prisoners, and encouraged exiles to return. **Democratic** elections did not take place in Guinea until 1993, when Conté, who had been head of the previous military regime, was again restored to power, despite accusations of ballot fraud. He was re-elected in 1998 and again in 2003. He remained in power until his death in 2008 after which Moussa Dadis Camera seized power in a coup and declared himself the head of a military junta. In 2009 soldiers brutally attacked a protest killing 157 people. Later that year Camera was shot in the head in an assassination attempt. Elections were eventually held in 2010 and won by Alpha Conde. Conde survived a coup attempt in 2011 and was re-elected in 2015.

Strong-arm government has nevertheless made Guinea relatively stable, despite economic

Text-Dependent Questions

1. What is Guinea's capital city?

2. What year did Guinea gain independence from France?

3. What are Guinea's important natural resources?

OPPOSITE: Dame de Mali in the Fouta Djalon mountains.

BELOW: The western chimpanzee (*Pan troglodytes verus*) is a subspecies of the common chimpanzee. It inhabits western Africa, mainly in Côte d'Ivoire and Guinea but has populations in surrounding countries. The species is currently endangered.

mismanagement. During the last decade, however, wars in neighboring Liberia and Sierra Leone have had their effect, causing an influx of refugees into the country and putting a strain on resources.

Guinea's Economy

The people of Guinea are some of the poorest in West Africa. Even though the country is potentially rich in minerals, agriculture employs 80 percent of the population. Most farming is at subsistence level. The climate is suitable for growing bananas, pineapples, cassava, rice, and coffee. Cattle and other livestock are raised in highland areas. Mineral resources include: bauxite (the most important export), iron ore, diamonds, gold, uranium, hydo-electricity, fish, and salt. The west coast of Africa is now ripe for oil development, and Guinea is a country that may well benefit.

GUINEA-BISSAU

A small republic on the coast of West Africa, Guinea-Bissau lies between Senegal and Guinea. The country is swampy, with many inland waterways and rainforests along its indented coast; it has low-lying **savanna** elsewhere. Offshore, the islands of the Bijagós **archipelago** have a culture all their own, as well as a diverse animal and marine wildlife.

The Portuguese explored the area in the 15th century when it became a center of the slave trade. Formerly Portuguese Guinea, it

Words to Understand

Archipelago: An expanse of water containing many scattered islands.

Bloodless coup: A revolution is sometimes described as bloodless — in these instances, political and revolutionary goals are achieved without any blood being shed or lives being lost.

Savanna: A large flat area of land with grass and very few trees, especially in Africa.

became a colony in 1879, winning independence from Portugal in 1974 after there had been guerrilla warfare involving the PAIGC (the African Party for the Independence of Guinea and Cape Verde) for over

OPPOSITE: A street in Bissau, the capital city.

RIGHT: The National People's Assembly of Guinea-Bissau.

BELOW: A map of Guinea-Bissau.

ten years. The first government, under Luis Cabral, was a single-party system with a planned economy. In 1980 there was a military coup in which João Vieira came to power, beginning the trend

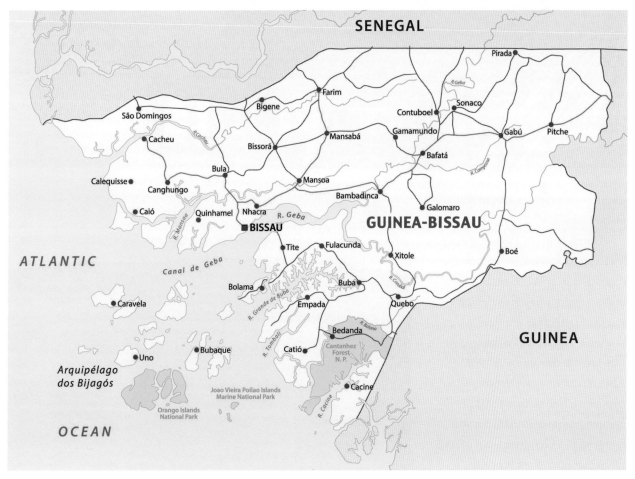

towards a muti-party system and a market economy.

Throughout the 1980s and early '90s, Vieira survived several abortive coups and in 1994 became president in the country's first free elections. His dismissal of his army chief, however, triggered a crippling civil war, and his overthrow in 1999. After an interim government, opposition leader Kumba Yalá became president in 2000, but was removed in a **bloodless coup** in 2003 when Henrique Rosa became

West African lion

The West African lion (*Panthera leo senegalensis*), also known as the Senegal lion, is subspecies native to western Africa. Their populations are small and fragmented and sadly are in great danger of extinction. The conservation of lions in West Africa has been largely neglected. The lions have a genetic sequence not found in other lions. If they are lost then a unique and locally adapted species will be lost forever.

OPPOSITE ABOVE: A traditionally-built Guinea-Bissau house.

OPPOSITE BELOW: Agriculture in Guineas-Bissau.

interim president. In 2005, former president Vieira returned from six years of exile in Portugal, winning back the presidency in the July 2005 elections. He was assassinated in 2009. Political instability and coup attempts followed. In May 2014 the presidential election was won by José Mário Vaz.

One of the poorest countries in the world, and one where income is most unequally distributed, Guinea-Bissau is dependent on farming and fishing for its survival, with cashews and rice its most important exports.

Peanuts, coconuts, pine nuts, and timber are also produced. Offshore oil prospecting is under way in several sectors but has not yet led to commercially viable deposits.

Text-Dependent Questions

1. What is Guinea-Bissau's capital city?

2. What European nation explored Guinea-Bissau in the 15th century?

3. What are Guinea-Bissau's main agricultural exports?

LIBERIA

Lying on the coast of the Atlantic Ocean between Sierra Leone and the Côte d'Ivoire, Liberia also has a land border with Guinea to the north-east. Lagoons and mangrove swamps line the flat coastal plain, which rises to a densely forested plateau with low mountains in the north-east. The main settlements are along the coast, where crops are cultivated.

Words to Understand

Corrupt: Having or showing a willingness to act dishonestly in return for money or personal gain.

Disarmament: The reduction or withdrawal of military forces and weapons.

Zero tolerance: Non-acceptance of antisocial behavior, typically by strict and uncompromising application of the law.

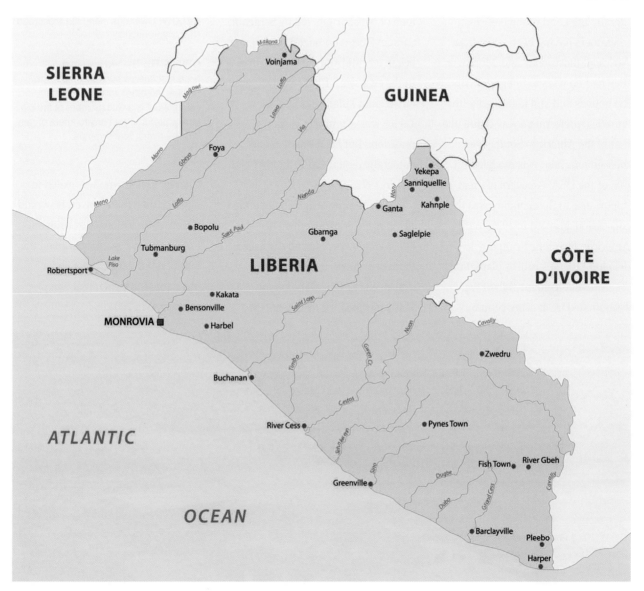

OPPOSITE: Bomi lake. Bomi is a county in north-west Liberia.

ABOVE: A map of Liberia.

Liberia's beginnings were in 1822, when a settlement was founded, near what is now Monrovia, by the American Colonization Society, as a home for Afro-American freed slaves. In 1847, these Americo-Liberians, as they were now known, declared the country's independence as the Republic of Liberia. This resulted in bitter struggles with the indigenous hostile tribes that lasted for many years and ultimately led to the coup of 1980 and successive civil wars.

However, the settlers regarded Liberia as their Promised Land, literally the Land of the Free, their forefathers having been taken from Africa all those years ago. Moreover, they had no wish to integrate with the natives and still identified with America, preferring a way of life like that of the American South; even their government was modeled on that of the USA. An event of great importance to the economy was the concession, granted in 1926, to the American Firestone Company to develop Liberia's rubber plantations.

In 1980 President Tolbert was assassinated in an army coup by men of tribal origin, led by Sergeant Samuel Doe, who seized control and began a brutal and **corrupt** regime. In the civil war of 1989–96, Doe was ousted and killed, and Charles Taylor was eventually elected president; but his repressive and autocratic regime led to another civil war in 1999.

In 2003 a peace agreement ended 14 years of civil war, which had killed 200,000 people and displaced thousands more. It had also destroyed the Liberian economy. This prompted the resignation of

BELOW: Dwellings along the Mesurado River, Monrovia.

OPPOSITE: The red river hog (*Potamochoerus porcus*) is native to Liberia and other western African countries. It is a wild member of the pig family, preferring an environment of rain forests, rivers, and swamps.

Charles Taylor, who was exiled to Nigeria, though he vowed he would return. A transitional government, under Gyude Bryant, was given the task of rebuilding Liberia and a program of **disarmament** was completed in 2004.

Ellen Johnson-Sirleaf, who was finance minister under President Tolbert in the late 1970s, was inaugurated as Africa's first elected woman president in January 2006, signaling a new time of hope. She faces the twin challenges of trying to rebuild the country and of fostering reconciliation. One of her priorities is to reintegrate former child soldiers into society, and she has declared "**zero tolerance**" of corruption. Johnson-Sirleaf was awarded the Nobel Peace Prize in 2011 and was also re-elected in the same year.

Liberia is heavily dependent on the export of iron, since it ceased to produce rubber in 1990. Now that sanctions have been lifted by the UN, it is once again an exporter of timber and diamonds. Liberia's infrastructure has been destroyed and the majority of the people are now unemployed and heavily dependent on foreign aid. An outbreak of Ebola hit Liberia in May 2014. It was the worst outbreak of the virus since it was identified 40 years ago.

Text-Dependent Questions

1. What did the American Colonization Society do in 1822?

2. Where are the majority of Liberia's crops cultivated?

3. What commodities are exported by Liberia today?

MALI

A landlocked country, Mali has borders with Algeria, Niger, Burkina Faso, Côte d'Ivoire, Guinea, Senegal, and Mauritania. Mali occupies the upper basins of the Senegal and Niger rivers, but for the most part consists of desert, with the Sahara lying to the north. The terrain is mostly flat, rising to undulating plains. There is savanna around the River Niger in the south, where most activity is centered, and where there is sufficient rain for cultivating crops.

Mali was one of the great medieval African empires, together with Ghana and Songhai, that grew to power in the Sahel (a vast semi-arid region south of the Sahara), all focused on the legendary city of Timbuktu. In the 14th century, Islam was adopted and Timbuktu became an important center of learning and trans-Saharan trade.

The present Mali was invaded by the French in 1880, when it became known as French Sudan. In 1959 the Mali **Federation** was born, following the union of Mali and Senegal. The federation gained independence from France in June 1960, but Senegal withdrew after only a few months. By September 1960, Mali had withdrawn

OPPOSITE: The Hand of Fatima is a rock formation near Hombori village. It is popular with climbers.

BELOW: A map of Mali.

Words to Understand

Federation: A country formed by separate states that have given certain powers to a central government while keeping control over local matters.

Natural resources: Materials or substances occurring in nature which can be exploited for economic gain.

Precipitate: To cause something to happen quickly or suddenly.

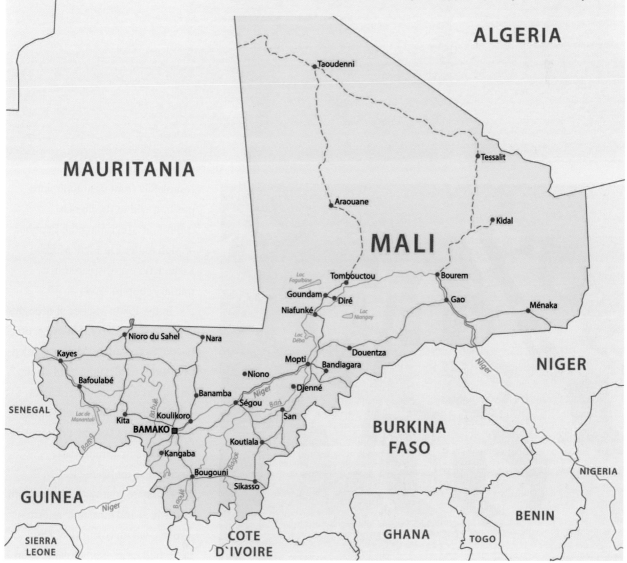

completely from its autonomous position within the French community, becoming the Republic of Mali under President Modibo Keïta, who was displaced in a military coup in 1968.

In the 1970s, a series of droughts caused the deaths of thousands of people from famine. Mali was ruled by a series of dictators until a coup prompted the formation of a new constitution in 1992, when Alpha Oumar Konaré became president after Mali's first multi-party elections. After his re-election in 1997, Konaré continued his program of political and economic reform – also his war on corruption. His permitted term of office came to an

OPPOSITE ABOVE: The Great Mosque of Djenné is located on the flood plain of the Bani River. The first mosque on the site was built around the 13th century, but the current structure dates from 1907.

OPPOSITE BELOW: Decorative details of a "mud" mosque in Saba in the Mopti region.

ABOVE: A view of Bamako, Mali's capital, with the Niger river in the background.

end in 2002, when he was succeeded by Amadou Toumani Touré, who had participated in the uprising of 1991 that had **precipitated** the adoption of democracy. Touré was subsequently elected for a second term in 2007.

In 2012, there was an uprising by Tuareg groups which led to unrest in the north. In that same year, the

Touré government was overthrown by the army. With the help of French troops, control over the north of the country was regained in 2013. After presidential polls, Ibrahim Boubacar Keita was sworn in as Mali's new president in 2013.

In 2015, Islamist gunmen attacked the Radisson Blu hotel in the capital Bamako.

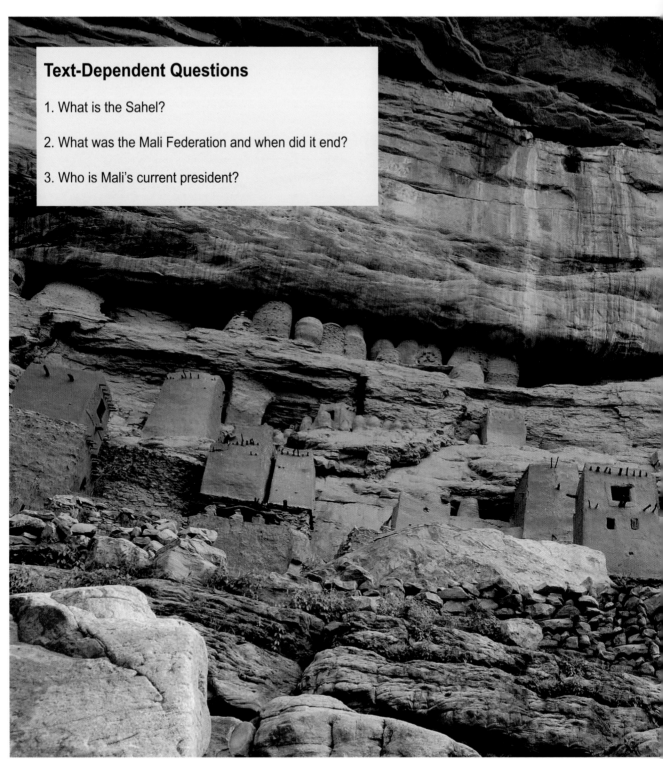

Text-Dependent Questions

1. What is the Sahel?

2. What was the Mali Federation and when did it end?

3. Who is Mali's current president?

Mali is rich in **natural resources**, yet is still one of the poorest countries in the world and heavily dependent on foreign aid. It has also suffered from the continued unrest in neighboring Côte d'Ivoire.

Bandiagara Escarpment

The Bandiagara Escarpment is situated in the Dogon country of Mali. It rises to 1,640 feet (500m) above sandy flats to the south.

The area of the escarpment is inhabited today by the Dogon people. Before the Dogon, the escarpment was inhabited by the Tellem and Toloy peoples up until the 15th century.

Today tourists groups can be escorted along the escarpment to visit the Dogon villages.

The Bandiagara Escarpment was listed in the UNESCO World Heritage List in 1989.

MAURITANIA

Situated in north-west Africa, over two-thirds of the Islamic Republic of Mauritania is covered by desert, much of it by the Sahara, and many of the people still lead **nomadic** lives, living by their flocks and herds. The rest of the population is concentrated in the south-western Sahel, many of them black Africans, with ethnic tensions existing between the minority black African and Arab-**Berber** populations to this day. The only agricultural land is a

LEFT: The Saudi Mosque or Grand Mosque in Nouakchott, the capital of Mauritania.

BELOW: Fishing boats on the beach beside the Atlantic Ocean at Port de Peche, Nouakchott.

OPPOSITE: A map of Mauritania.

relatively small area in the south along the Senegal river. Mauritania has a coastline on the Atlantic Ocean, where the capital, Nouakchott, is sited, and land

Words to Understand

Berber: A member of any of various peoples living in northern Africa west of Tripoli.

Nomadic: Roaming about from place to place, without a fixed pattern of movement.

Totalitarian: Controlling the people of a country in a very strict way with complete power that cannot be opposed.

borders with Western Sahara, Algeria, Mali, and Senegal.

The Romans called their African province Mauretania, after the Mauri or Berber people that inhabited the area. It continued to be the center of Berber power into the 11th and 12th centuries, when the Almoravid dynasty, which had established empires in Algeria, Morocco, and Spain, also brought Islam to the area. Nomadic Arab tribes became more dominant, while European trading posts sprang up along the coast.

Mauritania became a French protectorate in 1903 and a colony within French West Africa in 1920. It became fully independent within the French community in 1960, with Moktar Ould Daddah the first president of the one-party state.

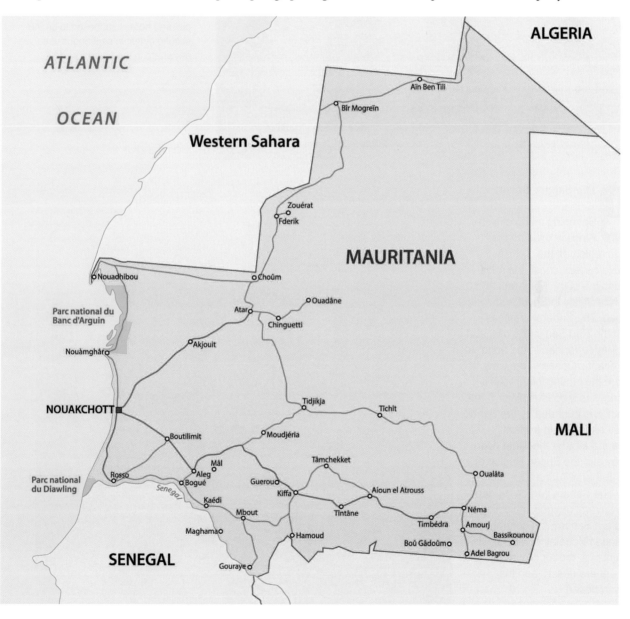

LEFT: Mauritanian boys studying at a Madrasah (Muslim school).

OPPOSITE: The Chinguetti Mosque in the heart of Chinguetti. It is an ancient center of worship created by the founders of the oasis city of Chinguetti in the Adrar region of Mauritania in the 13th or 14th century. The city's original purpose was to provide religious education to travelers.The minaret pictured here is supposed to be the second oldest in continuous use anywhere in the Muslim world.

The Sahara Desert

Spanning much of North Africa, excluding the fertile region on the Mediterranean coast, the Atlas Mountains of the Maghreb, and the Nile Valley in Egypt and Sudan. The Sahara stretches from the Red Sea in the east and the Mediterranean in the north, to the Atlantic Ocean in the west, where the landscape gradually changes to a coastal plain. To the south, it is bounded by the Sahel, a belt of semi-arid tropical savanna around the Niger river valley and the Sudan Region of sub-Saharan Africa.

The Sahara can be divided into several regions, including the western Sahara, the central Ahaggar Mountains, the Tibesti Mountains, the Aïr Mountains, the Ténéré desert, and the Libyan desert.

third, only to relinquish it three years later after being raided by Polisario guerillas seeking the independence of the territory.

Moktar Ould Daddah, the only president there had been since independence, was overthrown in a coup in 1978 and a military junta took control. In 1984 Maaouiya Ould Sid Ahmed Taya became president, still under a military regime. A new constitution and national assembly were adopted in 1991, with multi-party elections the following year. President Taya continued to preside, now over a civilian government, and later survived several attempts to oust him. However, on August 3, 2005, while he was in Saudi Arabia attending the funeral of the king, there was a bloodless coup, when the Military Council for Justice and Democracy, led by Ely Ould Mohamed Vall, seized power on the grounds that it was ending a **totalitarian** regime.

The first fully democratic presidential election since 1960 occurred on March 11, 2007, being the final transfer from military to civilian rule following the coup of 2005. It was won in a second round of voting by Sidi Ould, with Ahmed Ould Daddah coming a close second. The current president is Mohamed Ould Abdel Aziz who won the 2014 election.

Half the population still relies on its livestock and agriculture, though many abandoned the land for the cities after the repeated droughts of the 1970s and '80s. Mauritania has large deposits of iron ore, which make up nearly half of its exports. Other natural resources are gypsum, copper, phosphate, gold and diamonds, and reserves of oil and natural gas are under investigation. It also has some of the richest fishing waters off its coast, though overfishing is a concern. Recent tensions have arisen with Senegal over both countries' use of the Senegal river, that marks the border between the two.

Morocco opposed Mauritania's independence and for a time tried to absorb it. Matters improved, however, when King Hassan II of Morocco revealed his plan to divide Western Sahara. In 1976, Spain withdrew from the territory and Morocco took 66 percent of Western Sahara and Mauritania the southern

Text-Dependent Questions

1. What is the capital city of Mauritania?

2. When did Mauritania become a French protectorate?

3. Referring to the map, how many countries border Mauritania?

NIGER

A landlocked sub-Saharan country, Niger, that takes its name from the Niger river, is bordered by seven countries: Algeria, Libya, Chad, Nigeria, Benin, Burkina Faso, and Mali. Towards the center of the country, near Agadez, lie the semi-volcanic Aïr Mountains. Elsewhere, the terrain is predominantly desert with sand dunes, with hillier areas in the north and savanna, suitable for livestock and limited agriculture, in the south. It is hot, dusty and dry, and has a tropical climate in the extreme south.

The area that is now Niger was once occupied by powerful African empires, such as those of Mali and Songhai, and several northern Nigerian Hausa states also laid claims. During recent centuries, however, Tuareg nomads from the north have pushed southwards, clashing with the Fulani empire that had gained control of Hausa territory. In the 19th century, great travelers, such as Mungo Park and

BELOW: Looking across the Agadez skyline.

OPPOSITE: A map of Niger.

OPPOSITE BELOW: British explorer Mungo Park (1771–1806).

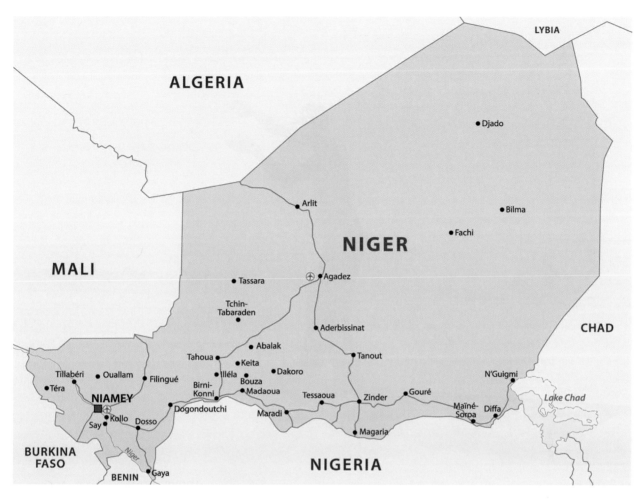

ALGERIA

LYBIA

• Djado

NIGER

• Arlit

• Bilma

• Fachi

MALI

• Tassara

 • Agadez

Tchin-
Tabaraden •

• Aderbissinat

CHAD

• Abalak

Tahoua •

• Tanout

• Keita

Tillabéri • • Ouallam Filingué •

• Illéla • Dakoro
Bouza

N'Guigmi •

• Téra

Birni-
Konni • • Madaoua

Lake Chad

NIAMEY

Dogondoutchi •

Tessaoua •

Zinder •

• Gouré

Maïné-
Soroa • Diffa •

Say • • Kollo Dosso

Maradi •

**BURKINA
FASO**

Niger

Magaria •

BENIN • Gaya

NIGERIA

Heinrich Barth began to explore the area in their search for the River Niger's source.

In 1922 Niger became a colony within French West Africa, becoming independent of France in 1960 when it was run by a single-party civilian regime under Hamani Diori. Devastating **drought** and allegations of corruption, however, led to a military coup in 1974, when Colonel Seyni Kountché took control, ruling the country until his death in 1987. He was succeeded by his chief-of-

staff, Ali Saibou, who was soon removed. A transitional government was installed in 1991 to pave the way for multi-party elections in 1993.

Meanwhile, the **Tuareg** had begun to agitate for greater autonomy. Rivalries within the coalition government, that was elected in the first fair and free elections in 1993, gave Colonel Ibrahim Baré Maïnassara a reason for overthrowing it in 1996, when he won a somewhat tarnished election. Unable to justify his coup, Baré

ABOVE: A Fisherman on the Niger River.

OPPOSITE ABOVE: Ancient rock art in Niger. Images carved and painted on natural rock depict vibrant scenes. Other examples can be found all over the Sahara.

ignored an international embargo against Libya, and looked to Libya for funds to help Niger's economy. This was followed by widespread violation of the civil liberties of opposition leaders, journalists, and others by an

was named head of a military government. However, in 2011 civilian rule was restored when Mahamadou Issoufou won the presidential election. He was re-elected in March 2016.

One of the poorest countries in the world, Niger's economy is based on subsistence agriculture, livestock, and some of the largest uranium reserves in the world, much of them going to France. However, a drop in world demand for uranium, together with the periods of prolonged drought not uncommon in the Sahel, together with a growing population, have taken their toll and Niger has to look to its camels, goats, cattle, and sheep for survival. It has difficulty feeding its people, due to the shortage of arable land, and relies heavily on food aid and other donations from abroad. There are thought to be reserves of oil, gold, phosphates, iron, and coal that Niger has insufficient funds to exploit, although the position may well change in the future.

unofficial militia composed of both police and military.

In the meantime, however, a 1995 peace accord was signed that ended the Tuareg insurgency in the north. In 1999, in a coup led by Major Daouda Malam Wanké, Baré was overthrown. A new constitution restored the semi-presidential system of government and led to the election of Mamadou Tandja as president in 1999; he was re-elected in 2004. In February 2010 President Tandja was ousted in a coup and senior army officer, Col. Salou Djibo

Text-Dependent Questions

1. Where does Niger get its name from?

2. What is the name of Niger's semi-volcanic mountain range?

3. What important natural resource is exported mainly to France?

NIGERIA

A country with a coastline on the Gulf of Guinea, Nigeria has land borders with Benin, Niger, and Cameroon. The south is hot and steamy around the delta of the Niger, which is a maze of creeks and mangrove swamps. Further inland is a belt of tropical forest that gives way to savanna, much of which has been cleared for farming. The terrain becomes increasingly treeless and arid towards the north; the Sokoto plains lie in the north-west, while to the south-east the rugged Adamawa Highlands extend along Nigeria's border with Cameroon.

Some of the most beautiful examples of African sculpture, thought to date from the Nok civilization that began in around 700 BC, have been excavated in the region. The Yoruba people date their presence in the area of modern Nigeria, Benin, and Togo to about 8500 BC, while the Kingdoms of Ife and Oyo, in the west of Nigeria, became prominent in about AD 700–900 and 1400–1835 respectively;

BELOW: Lagos is the largest city in Nigeria and is also an important port.

OPPOSITE: A map of Nigeria.

in the south-west, the power of the Kingdom of Benin prevailed between 1440 and 1897, and city-states proliferated under the Igbo, Hausa, and Fulani peoples.

In the 15th century, the Portuguese established trade with Benin, the area coming under British influence during the 19th century,

when the existing slave trade came to an end. By 1906 Britain had conquered all the country, dividing it into two protectorates, those of Northern and Southern Nigeria, the two merging into one in 1914. In 1954 Nigeria federated into three regions. Independence came in 1960 and the state became a federal republic within the Commonwealth.

Words to Understand

Imposition: The action or process of imposing something in an official way.

Junta: A military or political group that rules a country after taking power by force.

Tripartite: Shared by or involving three parties. "A tripartite coalition government."

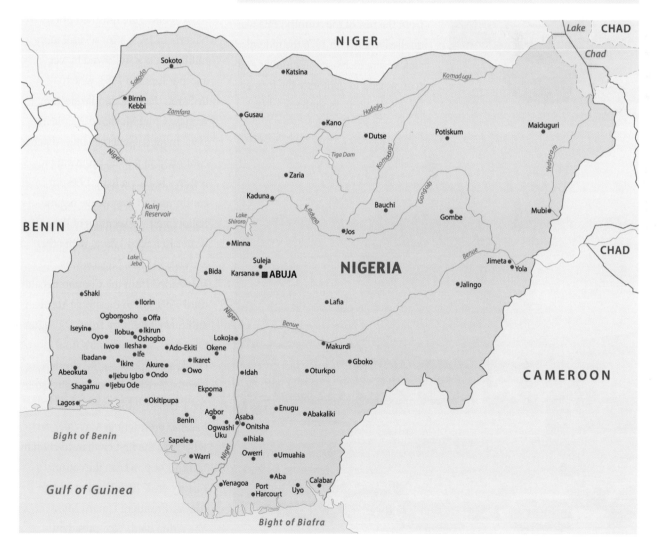

However, the **tripartite** arrangement was unable to contain rivalries – believed to be rooted in poverty, unemployment, and competition for land – between the 250 or so ethnic, linguistic, and religious groups that make up Nigeria – now Africa's most populous country. In 1966 a military coup by Igbo officers saw the start of a vicious civil war, when Biafra in the east attempted to split from the rest of the country; this was quelled in 1971. In 1976 the federal states were increased in number and reorganized to obliterate the former social divisions, though the

LEFT: A Bini mask, one of Nigeria's most recognized artifacts. Benin Empire, 16th century.

BELOW LEFT: The National Assembly, like many other parts of the Nigerian government, is based in the Federal Capital Territory, Abuja.

imposition of Islamic law in several states in 2000 was to cause thousands of Christians to flee.

Civilian rule returned briefly to Nigeria in 1979, after several more military coups, followed by yet another **junta** in 1983, which declared the presidential election, won by Chief Moshood Abiola in 1993, invalid. General Sanni Abacha continued in power, promising to restore civilian rule by 1998 but continuing an oppressive regime. Following the execution of the writer Ken Saro-Wiwa, with other activists in 1995, Nigeria was suspended from the Commonwealth until 1999, when the ethnic Yoruban and former military ruler, Olusegun Obasanjo, won Nigeria's first civilian-run presidential election for nearly 20 years. He was re-elected in 2003. Umaru Musa Yar'Adua became president in May 2007, in what was the first civilian-to-civilian transfer of power in the country's history. In 2010, following a long illness, President Umaru Musa Yar'Adua died. Vice-president

African Darter

African darter (*Anhinga rufa*), sometimes called the snakebird, is a water bird of sub-Saharan Africa where there are large bodies of water.

Goodluck Jonathan succeeded him and was formally elected as president in 2011. In March 2015 Muhammadu Buhari won the presidential election, bcoming the first opposition candidate to do so in Nigeria's history.

Oil had been discovered in the 1960s and '70s, when Nigeria emerged as one of the world's major producers. There have been undesirable side-effects, however, and the trade in stolen oil has fuelled violence, and revenues have been squandered through general corruption and mismanagement. Ethnic tensions and the growth of the Boko Haram militant group in the north-east has added to Nigeria's challenges. In early 2015 Nigeria, Chad, Cameroon, and Niger formed a military coalition against Boko Haram, claiming some successes.

Nigeria's food production has not been able to keep pace with the rapid population growth, with the result that food must now be imported.

Text-Dependent Questions

1. How long ago did the Yoruba people inhabit Nigeria ?

2. What year did Nigeria gain its independence?

3. What is Nigeria's most important natural resource?

SENEGAL

Senegal is the most westerly country in Africa. With a coastline on the Atlantic Ocean, it has land boundaries with Mauritania, Mali, Guinea, and Guinea-Bissau. Gambia forms a virtual **enclave** within Senegal, in a narrow strip that follows the Gambia river inland for 190 miles (300km). In the north of Senegal there is scrub and semi-desert, while the south is wetter and more fertile, rising to foothills in the south-east. It has several protected wildlife parks.

From the 10th to the 14th centuries, the Tukolor (Toucouleur) state of Tekrur dominated the area, though Senegal took its name from

BELOW: A map of Senegal.

OPPOSITE: Dakar is Senegal's capital. It is located on the Cap Vert peninsula on the Atlantic coast and is the westernmost city on the African mainland. Its position, on the western edge of Africa, is an advantageous departure point for trans-Atlantic and European trade; this fact aided its growth into a major regional port.

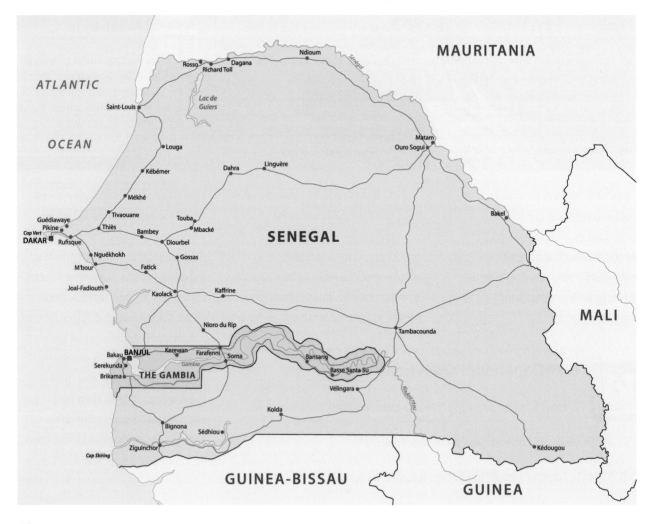

the Zenega Berbers, who brought Islam to the region in the 11th century from North Africa; it is still the dominant religion, though all religions and cultures are respected. Over the centuries, Senegal territory has been part of other West African major empires, including those of Mali and the Wolof. In the 1400s, the Portuguese reached Cape Verde and trading posts were opened. By the 17th century, the export trade in

Words to Understand

Enclave: A portion of territory or country surrounded by a larger territory or country.

Ethnic: Relating to a population subgroup (within a larger or dominant national or cultural group) with a common national or cultural tradition.

Separatist: A person who supports the separation of a particular group of people from a larger body on the basis of ethnicity or religion.

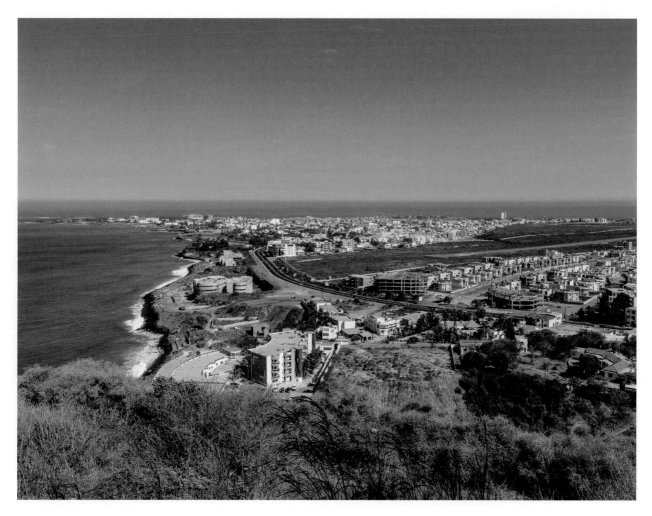

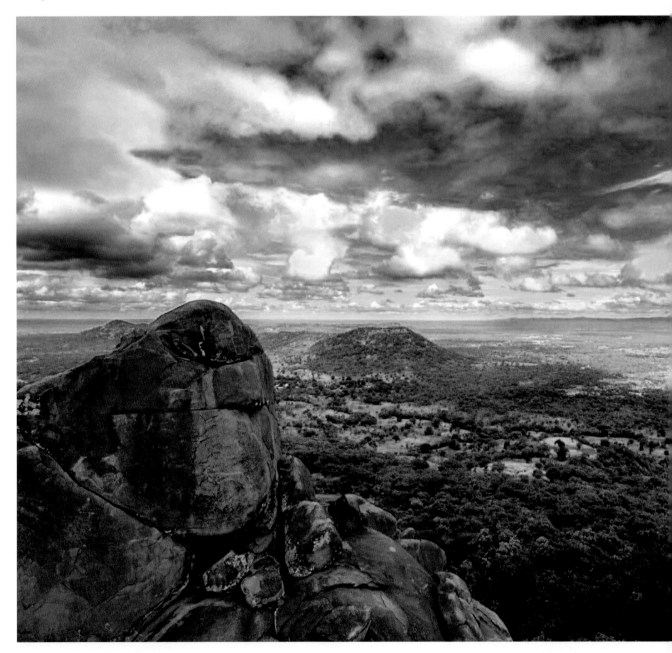

slaves, ivory and gold had been established by European traders, though the slave trade was dominated by the French from 1658, whose first colony was St.-Louis in the north-west. The French were temporarily expelled by the British in 1763, the British forming the colony of Senegambia, their first in Africa. The French regained control in 1783 and by 1902 Senegal was part of French West Africa. In 1946 it became French overseas territory, with representation in the French parliament.

Niokolo-Koba National Park

Niokolo-Koba National Park is a UNESCO World Heritage Site and natural protected area in south-eastern Senegal near the Guinea-Bissau border.

The park lies in an upland region through which the upper stretch of the Gambia river flows, towards the north-western border of Guinea. The park itself is arc-shaped running from the Upper Casamance/Kolda region at the Guinea-Bissau border into the Tambacounda region to within 62 miles (100km) of the Guinean border near the south-east corner of Senegal. Despite being protected, the park resources barely suffice to adequately protect its remaining wildlife.

1960 to 1980 was Léopold Sédar Senghor, a well-known poet and promoter of African culture, as well as a former campaigner for democracy. He was also a Senegalese deputy to the French National Assembly from 1946–58 and the founder of the Senegalese Progressive Union (UPS). He handed power over voluntarily to Abdou Diouf in 1980. In 1982, Senegal joined with Gambia to form the confederation of Senegambia, but the union was abandoned in 1989.

Since 1982 a long-running, low-level **separatist** war in the southern Casamance region has claimed hundreds of lives, though there have been hopes of peace since 2005; but armed clashes continued into 2006, prompting thousands of civilians to flee across the border into Gambia. The conflict concerns the Dioula people, who consider themselves marginalized by the Wolof, Senegal's main **ethnic** group.

The 40-year rule of Senegal's socialist government came to a

peaceful end in 2000, when Abdoulaye Wade of the Senegalese Democratic Party was elected president. In 2012, Macky Sall won elections to become the current president of Senegal. Mr Sall favors cutting the presidential term from seven years to five and limiting the number of consecutive terms a president can serve to two.

Senegal has a long history of international peace-keeping, having had a presence in the Democratic Republic of Congo, Liberia, and Kosovo. It also has a good political record of peaceful changes of leadership, and economic corruption is low. Therefore, although poverty is widespread and unemployment high, it is one of Africa's more stable economies. Agriculture is the main industry and peanuts, petroleum products, phosphates, and cotton are exported, while fishing is also important. It also has expanding information technology-based services.

Briefly a partner in the Federation of Mali (1959), Senegal withdrew and became a fully independent republic in 1960. Its first post-colonial president from

Text-Dependent Questions

1. What country does Senegal almost entirely surround?

2. What religion did the Zenega Berbers bring to Senegal?

3. What year did Senegal become fully independent?

SIERRA LEONE

Located between Guinea and Liberia, Sierra Leone has a coastline on the Atlantic Ocean to the south-west. The interior consists of forested **plateaux** and mountains to the east, while mangrove swamps line the coastal plain. To the north lies an area of tropical savanna.

Portuguese explorers arrived in 1460 and gave the area its name, having possibly been inspired by the mountainous peninsula of what is now Freetown, the capital.

In 1787, in an area that had previously been a source of slaves, a settlement for freed slaves was established at Freetown. Sierra Leone became a British crown colony in 1808, eventually gaining independence in 1961, with Sir Milton Margai its first prime minister. It was briefly a one-party state in the early 1980s.

The year 1991 saw the start of

the Sierra Leone Civil War, when the Revolutionary United Front (RUF) of Foday Sankoh, seeking to end foreign interference and nationalize the diamond mines, rebelled against the government. The result was tens of thousands of deaths, with the perpetrators of unspeakable **atrocities** eventually facing charges

of war crimes. Over 2 million people, well over a third of the population, were displaced, with many of them now living as refugees in neighboring countries.

Major Johnny Paul Koromah ousted the then-president, Ahmad Tejan Kabbah, in a military coup in 1997. In 1998 Kabbah was reinstated after the junta was overthrown by Nigerian-led intervention forces. In July 1999, a peace agreement, bolstered by peace-keeping forces, raised hopes that the country would rebuild its devastated economy and

Words to Understand

Atrocities: Very cruel or terrible acts or actions.

Infrastructure: The underlying foundation or basic framework in a system, country, or organization.

Plateaux: Large flat areas of land that are higher than other areas of land that surround it.

ABOVE: The road from Kenema to Kailahun District.

OPPOSITE: A map of Sierra Leone.

infrastructure. By the following year, however, the situation had deteriorated to such an extent that British troops were deployed to evacuate foreign nationals.

In 2002, Sierra Leone emerged from a decade of civil war, helped by Britain, UN peace-keepers, and financial contributions from abroad. The military, which assumed full responsibility for security following the departure of UN peace-keepers at the end of 2005, became a guarantor of the country's stability, but took a back seat during the 2007 election, when Ernest Bai Koroma was elected head of state; the country still looks to the UN,

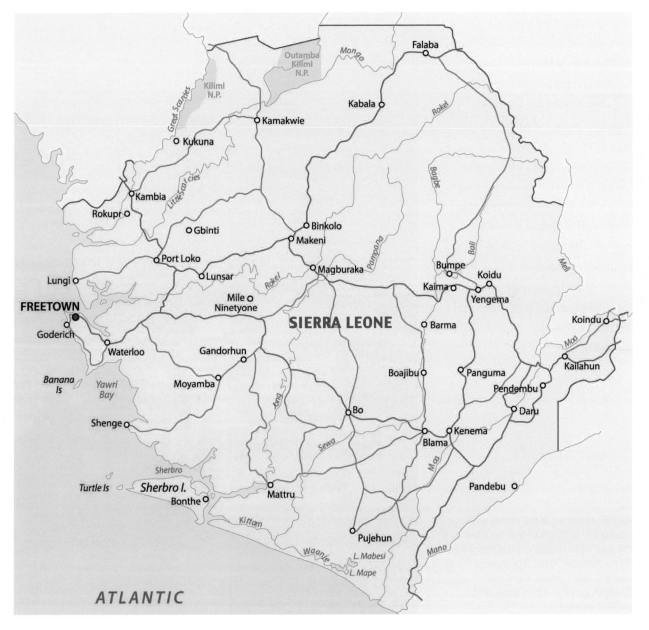

however, to support efforts to consolidate peace.

Sierra Leone is a poor country, and what wealth exists is not distributed fairly. It is now faced with the task of reconstruction, and the tribal rivalry and official corruption that led to the conflict have still not ended. The illicit trade in diamonds is known to have funded and perpetuated the war, and their mining has long been exploited at the expense of agriculture and industrial development, to the nation's cost. Diamond mining remains the major source of earnings, and represents nearly half of Sierra Leone's exports. The economic future of the country depends upon the maintenance of domestic peace and the continued receipt of substantial aid from abroad.

RIGHT: Freetown is the capital and largest city in Sierra Leone. Located in the west of the country, it is a major port on the Atlantic Ocean. Freetown is Sierra Leone's major urban, economic, financial, cultural, educational, and political center.

 Text-Dependent Questions

1. What European country gave Sierra Leone its name?

2. Who was Sierre Leone's first prime minister?

3. What year did the Sierre Leone Civil War start?

TOGO

Lying between Ghana and Benin, Togo also has a border with Burkina Faso to the north, and a short coastline on the Bight of Benin and the Gulf of Guinea to the south. It consists mainly of savanna grassland, divided by highland that crosses the country from north-east to south-west. There is a fertile plateau in the south, giving way to a marshy coastline with many lagoons.

The area was originally the province of Kwa and Voltaic peoples, with later influxes of Ewe and Mina clans from Nigeria, Ghana, and the Côte d'Ivoire. The slave trade flourished in the 16th century and several of the tribes, the

Words to Understand

Intimidation: To make someone afraid.

Nationalize: To cause something to be under the control of a national government.

Phosphate: A salt or compound that has phosphorus in it and that is used especially in products such as fertilizers that help plants grow.

Mina in particular, procured slaves for European traders. From 1884 to 1914, Togoland was a German protectorate, after a deal was made with the local king, Mlapa III, and cocoa, coffee, and cotton plantations were developed. During the First World War, Togoland was captured by Anglo-French forces and was divided between France and Britain when the war ended. It came under UN trusteeship from 1946 until 1956, when British Togoland chose to integrate with Ghana. In 1960 French Togoland chose independence as the Republic of Togo, with Sylvanus Oympio as its first president.

Togo was the first African country to undergo a military coup following independence: in 1963 Togolese veterans of the French army, many of whom had served in

LEFT: Wooden voodoo dolls in Akodessewa Fetish market in Lomé which is the largest in the world. Fetishes are objects such as statues or dried animal parts that are sold for their healing and spiritually rejuvenating properties.

OPPOSITE: A map of Togo.

Indo-China and Algeria, overthrew the president when he refused to let them join the Togolese army. Olympio was shot the next day by Sgt. Etienne Eyadéma, and Olympio's brother-in-law, Nicolas Grunitzky, assumed power. Grunitzky, however, was deposed in 1967 by Eyadéma, who became president in his place, allowing only one party, the Rassemblement du Peuple Togolais (RPT). After surviving what he believed to be an attempt on his life, he **nationalized** the phosphate mines and made all Togolese take African names, changing his own name to Gnassingbé Eyadéma.

From the late 1960s to 1980 Togo's economy boomed, thanks to phosphates, and Eyadéma's plans for Togo grew ever more grandiose, so that when recession came and the price of **phosphates** plummeted, the economy was left in tatters. There were many coup attempts thereafter. In the early 1990s there was international pressure for Eyadéma to democratize, which he resisted, and pro-democracy activists were brutally put down. This caused outrage at home and abroad and Eyadéma was forced to recapitulate; he was stripped of power and became president in name only. However, hardline tactics by the army, that was loyal to Eyadéma,

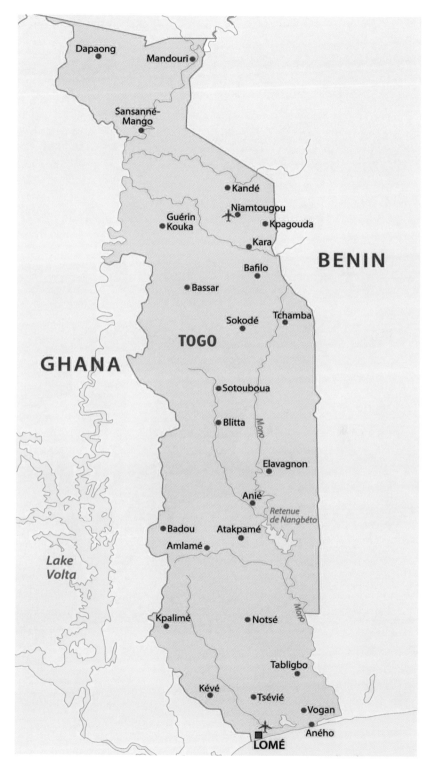

Text-Dependent Questions

1. Who were the original groups of people to inhabit Togo?

2. What year did French Togoland become the Republic of Togo?

3. What is Togo's most important cash crop?

continued and the transition to democracy came to a halt. Using blatant **intimidation**, Eyadéma somehow managed to claim most of the votes and was elected president again in 1993. By now the opposition seemed to have run out of steam, and Eyadéma held the reins as firmly as ever until 2005; at the time of his death later that year he was the longest-serving leader ever to have ruled in Africa. The speaker of the Togolese parliament should have succeeded him, but being temporarily absent, the army appointed Eyadéma's son, Faure Gnassingbé, as interim president, and elections were deferred to 2008. This caused uproar and he resigned, only to be elected president of Togo on April 24, 2005 and again in 2010. In September 2011, the president's half brother Kpatcha Gnassingbé was jailed for plotting to overthrow him. In 2013, the ruling party won the election with two-thirds of the votes. The opposition party, "Let's Save Togo" alleged irregularities. In

May 2015, the opposition candidate Jean-Pierre Fabre refused to recognize President Gnassingbé's election victories.

Togo relies heavily on agriculture and foreign aid. Cotton is the most important cash crop, but cocoa, and coffee are also exported. Togo is one of the world's largest producers of phosphates, though production has fallen over the last few years, owing to the cost of developing new deposits.

LEFT: The Nok and Mamproug Cave Dwellings are located in the Tandjouaré Prefecture in the Savanes Region of northern Togo. The Konkomba, Moba, and Mamprussi are among the peoples believed to have constructed the buildings.

Index

PHOTOGRAPHIC ACKNOWLEDGEMENTS

All images in this book are supplied under license from © Shutterstock.com other than the following: Wikimedia Commons and the following contributors:- Page 10: Peacecorpschadsey, page 24 below: Zenman, page 40 and 42 below: Jbdodane, page 41Colleen Taugher, page 64 above: Steve4710, page 64 below: Shiraz Chakera, Page 70: Lindsay Stark.

The content of this book was first published as *AFRICA*.

ABOUT THE AUTHOR
Annelise Hobbs

After completing her Classical studies, Annelise Hobbs became a librarian, working in a busy area of central London frequented by local authors and university students as well as the public itself. Eventually, she decided to use her extensive knowledge, and particularly her interest in travel, art, and architecture, to help in her research as an editor, inevitably progressing to writing books herself.

FIND OUT MORE:

Websites

- **Lonely Planet**
  www.lonelyplanet.com

- **Maps of Africa**
  www.worldatlas.com

- **National Geographic**
  travel.nationalgeographic.com

- **United Nations Educational, Scientific and Cultural Organization**
  http://whc.unesco.org

Further Reading by Mason Crest

AFRICA PROGRESS AND PROBLEMS
13 VOLUMES | 112 PAGES

Africa is a complex and diverse continent, and its more than 50 countries provide a study in contrasts: democracy and despotism, immense wealth and crushing poverty, modernism and traditionalism, peaceful communities and raging civil wars. The books in the AFRICA: PROGRESS AND PROBLEMS series take a close look at many of the major issues in Africa today, such as AIDS, poverty, government corruption, ethnic and religious tension, educational opportunities, and overcrowding. *2014 copyright*

THE EVOLUTION OF AFRICA'S MAJOR NATIONS
26 VOLUMES | 80 PAGES

Africa, with its rich natural resources and its incredible poverty, is a continent of contradictions. Each book in this series examines the historical and current situation of a particular African nation. Readers will learn about each country's history, geography, government, economy, cultures, and communities. *2013 copyright*